How to Get Rich Doing Business in China:

Key Country Guide for Businesses

By
Patrick W. Nee
(Patrick Nee)

The Internationalist®
www.internationalist.com

Titles Featured in the Business Guides Series

MAKING MONEY IN CHINA: Key Business Contacts and Addresses in China

MAKING MONEY IN CHINA: China Market Guide and Contacts

MAKING MONEY IN CHINA: China Country Guide for Businesses

HOW TO GET RICH DOING BUSINESS IN CHINA: China Country Guide for Businesses

The Internationalist®
International Business, Investment, and Travel

Published by:
The Internationalist Publishing Company
96 Walter Street/Suite 200
Boston MA 02131, USA
Tel: 617-354-7722
www.internationalist.com
PN@internationalist.com

Copyright © 2014 by PWN

The Internationalist is a Registered Trademark.
The Making Money in China series and The Internationalist Business Guides Series are Trademarks of the Internationalist Publishing Company/

All rights are reserved under International, Pan-American, and Pan-Asian Conventions. No part of this book may be reproduced in any form without the written permission of the publisher. All rights vigorously enforced.

Welcome to **How to Get Rich Doing Business in China.**:

The key to a successful business is knowing your client. HOW TO GET RICH DOING BUSINESS IN CHINA: KEY COUNTRY GUIDE FOR BUSINESSES offers executives, investors, and entrepreneurs the need-to-know information about doing business in China.

Written as an in-depth, straightforward reference guide, this book lists key information about Chinese people, culture, geography, history, government, and economy. A crucial list of key political personages also offers readers a short crash-course on the most current Chinese political landscape.

HOW TO GET RICH DOING BUSINESS IN CHINA: KEY COUNTRY GUIDE FOR BUSINESSES is a must-have reference book for anyone. Whether you are looking to break into international business or need to update your knowledge on China— this guide is for you.

The Internationalist

Contents

People
    Fast Facts:
    Ethnic Groups
    Language
    The Pinyin System of Romanization
    Religion
    Population Policy
Geography

History
    Dynastic Period
    Early 20th Century China
    The People's Republic of China
    The "Great Leap Forward" and the Sino-Soviet Split
    The Cultural Revolution
    The Post-Mao Era
    1989 Student Movement and Tiananmen Square
Government
    Chinese Communist Party
    State Structure
    Legal System
    Human Rights
Economy
    Economic Reforms
    Agriculture
    Industry
    Regulatory Environment
    Energy
    Environment
    Water
    Science and Technology
    Trade

- Foreign Investment
- Foreign Relations
- DEFENSE
- Nuclear Weapons
- Chemical Weapons
- Missiles

U.S- China Relations
- From Revolution to the Shanghai Communique
- Liaison Office, 1973-1978
- Normalization
- U.S.-China Relations since Normalization
- Bilateral Relations After Tiananmen
- U.S.-China Economic Relations
- U.S.-China Strategic and Economic Dialogue (S&ED)

Key Names and Contacts
- Principal Government and Party Officials
- American Diplomatic Representation in China
- Chinese Diplomatic Representation in the United States

People

Fast Facts:

- Nationality: Noun and adjective--Chinese (singular and plural).

-

    Population (July 2011 est.): 1,336,718,015.

- Population growth rate (2011 est.): 0.593%.

- Health (2010 est.): Infant mortality rate--16.06 deaths/1,000 live births. Life expectancy--74.68 years (overall); 72.68 years for males, 76.94 years for females.

- Ethnic groups (2000 census): Han Chinese 91.5%; Zhuang, Manchu, Hui, Miao, Uighur, Tujia, Yi, Mongol, Tibetan, Buyi, Dong, Yao, Korean, and other nationalities 8.5%.

- Religions (2002 est.): Officially atheist; Daoist (Taoist), Buddhist, Christian, Muslim.

- Language: Official--Mandarin (Putonghua); there also are many local dialects.

- Education: Years compulsory--9. Literacy--92.2%.

- Total labor force (2010 est.): 780 million.

- Labor force by occupation (2008 est.): Primary (agriculture)--297.08 million, 38.1%;secondary (industrial)--216.84 million, 27.8%; tertiary (services)--266.03 million, 34.1%.

Ethnic Groups

The largest ethnic group is the Han Chinese, who constitutes about 91.5% of the total population (2000 census). The remaining 8.5% are Zhuang (16 million), Manchu (10 million), Hui (9 million), Miao (8 million), Uighur (7 million), Yi (7 million), Mongol (5 million), Tibetan (5 million), Buyi (3 million), Korean (2 million), and other ethnic minorities.

Language

There are seven major Chinese dialects and many sub dialects. Mandarin (or Putonghua), the predominant dialect, is spoken by over 70% of the population. It is taught in all schools and is the medium of government. About two-thirds of the Han ethnic group are native speakers of Mandarin; the rest, concentrated in southwest and southeast China, speak one of the six other major Chinese dialects. Non-Chinese languages spoken widely by ethnic minorities include Mongolian, Tibetan, Uighur and other Turkic languages (in Xinjiang), and Korean (in the northeast). Some autonomous regions and special administrative regions have their own official languages. For example, Mongolian has official status within the Inner Mongolian Autonomous Region of China.

The Pinyin System of Romanization

On January 1, 1979, the Chinese Government officially adopted the pinyin system for spelling Chinese names and places in Roman letters. A system of Romanization invented by the Chinese, pinyin has long been widely used in China on street and commercial signs as well as in elementary Chinese textbooks as an aid in learning Chinese characters. Variations of pinyin also are used as the written forms of several minority languages.

Pinyin has now replaced other conventional spellings in China's

English-language publications. The U.S. Government also has adopted the pinyin system for all names and places in China. For example, the capital of China is now spelled "Beijing" rather than "Peking."

Religion

A February 2007 survey conducted by East China Normal University and reported in state-run media concluded that 31.4% of Chinese citizens ages 16 and over are religious believers. While the Chinese constitution affirms "freedom of religious belief," the Chinese Government places restrictions on religious practice, particularly on religious practice outside officially recognized organizations. The five state-sanctioned "patriotic religious associations" are Buddhism, Taoism, Islam, Catholicism, and Protestantism. Buddhism is most widely practiced; the state-approved Xinhua news agency estimates there are 100 million Buddhists in China. According to the State Administration for Religious Affairs (SARA), there are more than 21 million Muslims in the country. Christians on the mainland number nearly 23 million, accounting for 1.8% of the population, according to The Blue Book of Religions (compiled by the Chinese Academy of Social Sciences' Institute of World Religions and released in August 2010). Other official figures indicate there are 5.3 million Catholics, though unofficial estimates are much higher. The Pew Research Center estimated in 2007 that 50 million to 70 million Christians practice in unregistered religious gatherings or "house" churches. There are no official statistics confirming the number of Taoists in China.

Although officially restricted from 1949 until the 1980s, Buddhism has regained popularity in China and has become the largest organized religion in the country. There continue to be strict government restrictions on Tibetan Buddhism.

Of China's 55 officially recognized minorities, 10 groups are predominately Muslim. According to government figures, there are 36,000 Islamic places of worship and more than 45,000 imams.

Only two Christian organizations--a "patriotic" Catholic association without official ties to Rome and the "Three-Self-Patriotic" Protestant church--are sanctioned by the Chinese Government. Unregistered "house" churches exist in many parts of the country. The extent to which local authorities have tried to control the activities of unregistered churches varies from region to region. However, the government suppresses the religious activities of "underground" Roman Catholic clergy who are not affiliated with the official patriotic Catholic association and have avowed loyalty to the Vatican, which the government accuses of interfering in the country's internal affairs. The government also severely restricts the activities of groups it designates as "evil cults," including several Christian groups and the Falun Gong spiritual movement.

Population Policy

With a population officially over 1.3 billion and an estimated population growth rate of 0.593% (2011 est.), China is very concerned about its population growth and has attempted with mixed results to implement a strict birth limitation policy. China's 2002 Population and Family Planning Law and policy permits one child per family, with allowance for a second child under certain circumstances, especially in rural areas, and with guidelines looser for ethnic minorities with small populations. Enforcement varies and relies largely on "social compensation fees" to discourage extra births. Official government policy prohibits the use of physical coercion to compel persons to submit to abortion or sterilization, but in some localities there are instances of local birth-planning officials using physical coercion to meet birth limitation targets. The government's goal is to stabilize the population in the first half of the 21st century, and 2009 projections from the U.S. Census Bureau were that the Chinese population would peak at around 1.4 billion by 2026.

Geography

- Total area: 9,596,961 sq. km. (about 3.7 million sq. mi.).

- Capital--Beijing.

- Other major cities--Shanghai, Tianjin, Shenyang, Shenzhen, Wuhan, Guangzhou, Chongqing, Harbin, Chengdu, and Dalian.

- Terrain: Plains, deltas, and hills in east; mountains, high plateaus, deserts in west.

- Climate: Tropical in south to subarctic in north.

History

Dynastic Period

China is the oldest continuous major world civilization, with records dating back about 3,500 years. Successive dynasties developed a system of bureaucratic control that gave the agrarian-based Chinese an advantage over neighboring nomadic and hill cultures. Chinese civilization was further strengthened by the development of a Confucian state ideology and a common written language that bridged the gaps among the country's many local languages and dialects. Whenever China was conquered by nomadic tribes, as it was by the Mongols in the 13th century, the conquerors sooner or later adopted the ways of the "higher" Chinese civilization and staffed the bureaucracy with Chinese.

The last dynasty was established in 1644, when the Manchus overthrew the native Ming dynasty and established the Qing

(Ch'ing) dynasty with Beijing as its capital. At great expense in blood and treasure, the Manchus over the next half-century gained control of many border areas, including Xinjiang, Yunnan, Tibet, Mongolia, and Taiwan. The success of the early Qing period was based on the combination of Manchu martial prowess and traditional Chinese bureaucratic skills.

During the 19th century, Qing control weakened, and prosperity diminished. China suffered massive social strife, economic stagnation, explosive population growth, and Western penetration and influence. The Taiping and Nian rebellions, along with a Russian-supported Muslim separatist movement in Xinjiang, drained Chinese resources and almost toppled the dynasty. Britain's desire to continue its opium trade with China collided with imperial edicts prohibiting the addictive drug, and the First Opium War erupted in 1840. China lost the war; subsequently, Britain and other Western powers, including the United States, forcibly occupied "concessions" and gained special commercial privileges. Hong Kong was ceded to Britain in 1842 under the Treaty of Nanking, and in 1898, when the Opium Wars finally ended, Britain executed a 99-year lease of the New Territories, significantly expanding the size of the Hong Kong colony.

As time went on, the Western powers, wielding superior military technology, gained more economic and political privileges. Reformist Chinese officials argued for the adoption of Western technology to strengthen the dynasty and counter Western advances, but the Qing court played down both the Western threat and the benefits of Western technology.

Early 20th Century China

Frustrated by the Qing court's resistance to reform, young officials, military officers, and students--inspired by the revolutionary ideas of Sun Yat-sen--began to advocate the overthrow of the Qing dynasty and creation of a republic. A revolutionary military uprising on October 10, 1911, led to the abdication of the last Qing monarch. As part of a compromise to overthrow the dynasty without a civil war, the revolutionaries and reformers allowed high Qing officials to retain prominent positions in the new republic. One of these figures, Gen. Yuan Shikai, was chosen as the republic's first president. Before his death in 1916, Yuan unsuccessfully attempted to name himself emperor. His death left the republican government all but shattered, ushering in the era of the "warlords" during which China was ruled and ravaged by shifting coalitions of competing provincial military leaders.

In the 1920s, Sun Yat-sen established a revolutionary base in south China and set out to unite the fragmented nation. With Soviet assistance, he organized the Kuomintang (KMT or "Chinese Nationalist People's Party"), and entered into an alliance with the fledgling Chinese Communist Party (CCP). After Sun's death in 1925, one of his proteges, Chiang Kai-shek, seized control of the KMT and succeeded in bringing most of south and central China under its rule. In 1927, Chiang turned on the CCP and executed many of its leaders. The remnants fled into the mountains of eastern China. In 1934, driven out of their mountain bases, the CCP's forces embarked on a "Long March" across some of China's most desolate terrain to the northwestern province of Shaanxi, where they established a guerrilla base at Yan'an.

During the "Long March," the communists reorganized under a new leader, Mao Zedong (Mao Tse-tung). The bitter struggle between the KMT and the CCP continued openly or clandestinely through the 14-year-long Japanese invasion (1931-45), even though the two parties nominally formed a united front to oppose the Japanese invaders in 1937. The war between the two parties resumed after the Japanese defeat in 1945. By 1949, the CCP occupied most of the country.

Chiang Kai-shek fled with the remnants of his KMT government and military forces to Taiwan, where he proclaimed Taipei to be China's "provisional capital" and vowed to re-conquer the Chinese mainland. Taiwan still calls itself the "Republic of China."

The People's Republic of China

In Beijing, on October 1, 1949, Mao Zedong proclaimed the founding of the People's Republic of China (P.R.C.). The new government assumed control of a people exhausted by two generations of war and social conflict, and an economy ravaged by high inflation and disrupted transportation links. A new political and economic order modeled on the Soviet example was quickly installed.

In the early 1950s, China undertook a massive economic and social reconstruction program. The new leaders gained popular support by curbing inflation, restoring the economy, and rebuilding many war-damaged industrial plants. The CCP's authority reached into almost every aspect of Chinese life. Party control was assured by large, politically loyal security and military forces; a government apparatus responsive to party direction; and the placement of party members in leadership positions in labor, women's, and other mass organizations.

The "Great Leap Forward" and the Sino-Soviet Split

In 1958, Mao broke with the Soviet model and announced a new economic program, the "Great Leap Forward," aimed at rapidly raising industrial and agricultural production. Giant cooperatives (communes) were formed, and "backyard factories" dotted the Chinese landscape. The results were disastrous. Normal market mechanisms were disrupted, agricultural production fell behind, and China's people exhausted themselves producing what turned out to be shoddy, un-salable goods. Within a year, starvation appeared even in fertile agricultural areas. From 1960 to 1961, the combination of poor planning during the Great Leap Forward and bad weather resulted in one of the deadliest famines in human history.

The already-strained Sino-Soviet relationship deteriorated sharply in 1959, when the Soviets started to restrict the flow of scientific and technological information to China. The dispute escalated, and the Soviets withdrew all of their personnel from

China in August 1960. In 1960, the Soviets and the Chinese began to have disputes openly in international forums.

The Cultural Revolution

In the early 1960s, State President Liu Shaoqi and his protege, Party General Secretary Deng Xiaoping, took over direction of the party and adopted pragmatic economic policies at odds with Mao's revolutionary vision. Dissatisfied with China's new direction and his own reduced authority, Party Chairman Mao launched a massive political attack on Liu, Deng, and other pragmatists in the spring of 1966. The new movement, the "Great Proletarian Cultural Revolution," was unprecedented in communist China's history. For the first time, a section of the Chinese communist leadership sought to rally popular opposition against another leadership group. China was set on a course of political and social anarchy that lasted the better part of a decade.

In the early stages of the Cultural Revolution, Mao and his "closest comrade in arms," National Defense Minister Lin Biao, charged Liu, Deng, and other top party leaders with dragging China back toward capitalism. Radical youth organizations, called Red Guards, attacked party and state organizations at all levels, seeking out leaders who would not bend to the radical wind. In reaction to this turmoil, some local People's Liberation Army (PLA) commanders and other officials maneuvered to outwardly back Mao and the radicals while actually taking steps to rein in local radical activity.

Gradually, Red Guard and other radical activity subsided, and the Chinese political situation stabilized along complex factional lines. The leadership conflict came to a head in September 1971, when Party Vice Chairman and Defense Minister Lin Biao reportedly tried to stage a coup against Mao; Lin Biao allegedly later died in a plane crash in Mongolia.

In the aftermath of the Lin Biao incident, many officials criticized and dismissed during 1966-69 were reinstated. Chief among these was Deng Xiaoping, who reemerged in 1973 and was confirmed in 1975 in the concurrent posts of Party Vice Chairman, Politburo Standing Committee member, PLA Chief of Staff, and Vice Premier.

The ideological struggle between more pragmatic, veteran party officials and the radicals re-emerged with a vengeance in late 1975. Mao's wife, Jiang Qing, and three close Cultural Revolution associates (later dubbed the "Gang of Four") launched a media campaign against Deng. In January 1976, Premier Zhou Enlai, a popular political figure, died of cancer. On April 5, Beijing citizens staged a spontaneous demonstration in Tiananmen Square in Zhou's memory, with strong political overtones of support for Deng. The authorities forcibly suppressed the demonstration. Deng was blamed for the disorder and stripped of all official positions, although he retained his party membership.

The Post-Mao Era

Mao's death in September 1976 removed a towering figure from Chinese politics and set off a scramble for succession. Former Minister of Public Security Hua Guofeng was quickly confirmed as Party Chairman and Premier. A month after Mao's death, Hua, backed by the PLA, arrested Jiang Qing and other members of the "Gang of Four." After extensive deliberations, the Chinese Communist Party leadership reinstated Deng Xiaoping to all of his previous posts at the 11th Party Congress in August 1977. Deng then led the effort to place government control in the hands of veteran party officials opposed to the radical excesses of the previous 2 decades.

The new, pragmatic leadership emphasized economic development and renounced mass political movements. At the pivotal December 1978 Third Plenum (of the 11th Party Congress Central Committee), the leadership adopted economic reform policies aimed at expanding rural income and incentives, encouraging experiments in enterprise autonomy, reducing central planning, and attracting foreign direct investment to China. The plenum also decided to accelerate the pace of legal reform, culminating in the passage of several new legal codes by the National People's Congress in June 1979.

After 1979, the Chinese leadership moved toward more pragmatic positions in almost all fields. The party encouraged artists, writers, and journalists to adopt more critical approaches, although open attacks on party authority were not permitted. In late 1980, Mao's Cultural Revolution was officially proclaimed a catastrophe. Hua Guofeng, a protege of Mao, was replaced as premier in 1980 by reformist Sichuan party chief Zhao Ziyang and as party General Secretary in 1981 by the even more reformist Communist Youth League chairman Hu Yaobang.

Reform policies brought great improvements in the standard of living, especially for urban workers and for farmers who took advantage of opportunities to diversify crops and establish village industries. Controls on literature and the arts were relaxed, and Chinese intellectuals established extensive links with scholars in other countries.

At the same time, however, political dissent as well as social problems such as inflation, urban migration, and prostitution emerged. Although students and intellectuals urged greater reforms, some party elders increasingly questioned the pace and the ultimate goals of the reform program. In December 1986, student demonstrators, taking advantage of the loosening political atmosphere, staged protests against the slow pace of reform, confirming party elders' fear that the current reform program was leading to social instability. Hu Yaobang, a protege of Deng and a leading advocate of reform, was blamed for the protests and forced to resign as CCP General Secretary in January 1987. Premier Zhao Ziyang was made General Secretary and Li Peng, former Vice Premier and Minister of Electric Power and Water Conservancy, was made Premier.

1989 Student Movement and Tiananmen Square

After Zhao became the party General Secretary, the economic and political reforms he had championed, especially far-reaching political reforms enacted at the 13th Party Congress in the fall of 1987 and subsequent price reforms, came under increasing attack. His proposal in May 1988 to accelerate price reform led to widespread popular complaints about rampant inflation and gave opponents of rapid reform the opening to call for greater centralization of economic controls and stricter prohibitions against Western influence. This precipitated a political debate, which grew more heated through the winter of 1988-89.

The death of Hu Yaobang on April 15, 1989, coupled with growing economic hardship caused by high inflation, provided the backdrop for a large-scale protest movement by students, intellectuals, and other parts of a disaffected urban population. University students and other citizens camped out in Beijing's Tiananmen Square to mourn Hu's death and to protest against those who would slow reform. Their protests, which grew despite government efforts to contain them, called for an end to official corruption, a greater degree of democracy, and for defense of freedoms guaranteed by the Chinese constitution. Protests also spread to many other cities, including Shanghai, Chengdu, and Guangzhou.

Martial law was declared on May 20, 1989. Late on June 3 and early on the morning of June 4, military units were brought into Beijing. They used armed force to clear demonstrators from the streets. There are no official estimates of deaths in Beijing, but most observers believe that casualties numbered in the hundreds.

After June 4, while foreign governments expressed horror at the brutal suppression of the demonstrators, the central government eliminated remaining sources of organized opposition, detained large numbers of protesters, and required political reeducation not only for students but also for large numbers of party cadre and government officials. Zhao was purged at the Fourth Plenum of the 13th Central Committee in June and replaced as

Party General Secretary by Jiang Zemin. Deng's power was curtailed as more orthodox party leaders, led by Chen Yun, became the dominant group in the leadership.

Following this resurgence of conservatives in the aftermath of June 4, economic reform slowed until given new impetus by Deng Xiaoping's return to political dominance 2 years later, including a dramatic visit to southern China in early 1992. Deng's renewed push for a market-oriented economy received official sanction at the 14th Party Congress later in the year as a number of younger, reform-minded leaders began their rise to top positions. Hu Jintao was elevated to the Politburo Standing Committee at the Congress. Deng and his supporters argued that managing the economy in a way that increased living standards should be China's primary policy objective, even if "capitalist" measures were adopted. Subsequent to the visit, the Communist Party Politburo publicly issued an endorsement of Deng's policies of economic openness. Though continuing to espouse political reform, China has consistently placed overwhelming priority on the opening of its economy.

Post-Deng Leadership

Deng's health deteriorated in the years prior to his death in 1997. During that time, Party General Secretary and P.R.C. President Jiang Zemin and other members of his generation gradually assumed control of the day-to-day functions of government. This "third generation" leadership governed collectively with Jiang at the center.

In the fall of 1987, Jiang was re-elected Party General Secretary at the 15th Party Congress, and in March 1998 he was re-elected President during the 9th National People's Congress. Premier Li Peng was constitutionally required to step down from that post. He was elected to the chairmanship of the National People's Congress. The reform-minded pragmatist Zhu Rongji was selected to replace Li as Premier.

In November 2002, the 16th Communist Party Congress elected Hu Jintao as the new General Secretary. In 1992 Deng Xiaoping had informally designated Hu Jintao as the leading figure among the "fourth generation" leaders. A new Politburo and Politburo Standing Committee was also elected in November.

In March 2003, General Secretary Hu Jintao was elected President at the 10th National People's Congress. Jiang Zemin retained the chairmanship of the Central Military Commission. At the Fourth Party Plenum in September 2004, Jiang Zemin retired from the Central Military Commission, passing the Chairmanship and control of the People's Liberation Army to President Hu Jintao.

The Chinese Communist Party's 17th Party Congress, held in October 2007, saw the elevation of key "fifth generation" leaders to the Politburo and Standing Committee, including Xi Jinping, Li Keqiang, Li Yuanchao, and Wang Yang. At the National People's Congress plenary held in March 2008, Xi was elected Vice President of the government, and Li Keqiang was elected Vice Premier. The 18th Party Congress is scheduled to be held in the fall of 2012. It is expected that President Hu Jintao, in keeping with precedent, will step down as the party's General Secretary at that time, and the Congress will elect the 18th Central Committee of the Communist Party of China.

Government

- Type: Communist party-led state.

- Constitution: December 4, 1982; revised several times, most recently in 2004.

- Independence: Unification under the Qin (Ch'in) Dynasty 221 BC; Qing (Ch'ing or Manchu) Dynasty replaced by a republic on February 12, 1912; People's Republic established October 1, 1949.

- Branches: *Executive*--president, vice president, State Council, premier. *Legislative*--unicameral National People's Congress. *Judicial*--Supreme People's Court, Local People's Courts, Special People's Courts.

- Administrative divisions: 23 provinces (the P.R.C. considers Taiwan to be its 23rd province); 5 autonomous regions, including Tibet; 4 municipalities directly under the State Council.

- Political parties: Chinese Communist Party, 76 million members; 8 minor parties under Communist Party supervision.

Chinese Communist Party

The estimated 78 million-member CCP, authoritarian in structure and ideology, continues to dominate government. Nevertheless, China's population, geographical vastness, and social diversity frustrate attempts to rule by fiat from Beijing. Central leaders must increasingly build consensus for new policies among party members, local and regional leaders, influential non-party members, and the population at large.

In periods of greater openness, the influence of people and organizations outside the formal party structure has tended to increase, particularly in the economic realm. This phenomenon is most apparent today in the rapidly developing coastal region. Nevertheless, in all important government, economic, and cultural institutions in China, party committees work to see that party and state policy guidance is followed and that non-party members do not create autonomous organizations that could challenge party rule. Party control is tightest in government offices and in urban economic, industrial, and cultural settings;

it is considerably looser in the rural areas, where roughly half of the people live.

Theoretically, the party's highest body is the Party Congress, which traditionally meets at least once every 5 years. The 17th Party Congress took place in fall 2007. The primary organs of power in the Communist Party include:

- The Politburo Standing Committee, which currently consists of nine members
- The Politburo, consisting of 25 full members, including the members of the Politburo Standing Committee
- The Secretariat, the principal administrative mechanism of the CCP, headed by Politburo Standing Committee member and executive secretary Xi Jinping
- The Central Military Commission, charged with rooting out corruption and malfeasance among party cadres.

State Structure

The Chinese Government has always been subordinate to the Chinese Communist Party; its role is to implement party policies. The primary organs of state power are the National People's Congress (NPC), the President (the head of state), and the State Council. Members of the State Council include Premier Wen Jiabao (the head of government), a variable number of vice premiers (now four), five state councilors (protocol equivalents of vice premiers but with narrower portfolios), and 25 ministers, the central bank governor, and the auditor-general.

Under the Chinese constitution, the NPC is the highest organ of state power in China. It meets annually for about 2 weeks to review and approve major new policy directions, laws, the budget, and major personnel changes. These initiatives are presented to the NPC for consideration by the State Council after previous endorsement by the Communist Party's Central Committee. Although the NPC generally approves State Council policy and personnel recommendations, various NPC committees hold active debate in closed sessions, and changes may be made to accommodate alternative views.

When the NPC is not in session, its permanent organ, the Standing Committee, exercises state power.

Legal System

The government's efforts to promote rule of law are ongoing. After the Cultural Revolution, China's leaders aimed to develop a legal system to restrain abuses of official authority and revolutionary excesses. In 1982, the National People's Congress adopted a new state constitution that emphasized the rule of law under which even party leaders are theoretically held accountable.

Since 1979, when the drive to establish a functioning legal system began, more than 300 laws and regulations, most of them in the economic area, have been promulgated. The use of mediation committees--informed groups of citizens who resolve about 90% of China's civil disputes and some minor criminal cases at no cost to the parties--is one innovative device. There are more than 800,000 such committees in both rural and urban areas.

Legal reform became a government priority in the 1990s. Legislation designed to modernize and professionalize the nation's lawyers, judges, and prisons was enacted. The 1994 Administrative Procedure Law allows citizens to sue officials for abuse of authority or malfeasance. In addition, the criminal law and the criminal procedures laws were amended to introduce significant reforms. The criminal law amendments abolished the crime of "counter-revolutionary" activity, although many persons are still incarcerated for that crime. Criminal procedures reforms also encouraged establishment of a more transparent, adversarial trial process. The Chinese constitution and laws provide for fundamental human rights, including due process, but these are often ignored in practice. In addition to other judicial reforms, the constitution was amended in 2004 to include the protection of individual human rights and legally-obtained private property, but it is unclear how some of these provisions will be implemented. Since this amendment, there have been new publications in bankruptcy law and anti-monopoly law, and modifications to company law and labor law. Although new criminal and civil laws have provided additional safeguards to citizens, previously debated political reforms, including expanding elections to the township level beyond the current trial basis, have been put on hold.

Human Rights

The State Department's 2010 Human Rights Practices and International Religious Freedom Reports noted China's continuing abuses of human rights in violation of internationally recognized norms, stemming both from the authorities' intolerance of dissent and the inadequacy of legal safeguards for basic freedoms. The government has increased its efforts to reign in civil society, particularly non-governmental organizations (NGOs) involved in rights advocacy and public interest issues, and has stepped up attempts to limit freedom of speech and freedom of religion and to control the press, the Internet, and Internet access. Abuses increased around high-profile events in 2010, such as the awarding of the Nobel Peace Prize to democracy activist Liu Xiaobo and the anniversaries of the 1959 Tibetan uprising, the Tiananmen Square incident, and the founding of the People's Republic of China. The government continued its severe cultural and religious repression of ethnic minorities in the Xinjiang Uighur Autonomous Region (XUAR) and Tibetan areas. Other reported abuses included arbitrary and lengthy incommunicado detention, extrajudicial killings, executions without due process, forced confessions, torture, and mistreatment of prisoners as well as severe restrictions on freedom of speech, the press, assembly, association, religion, privacy, worker rights, and coercive birth limitation. China continues the monitoring, harassment, intimidation, and arrest of journalists, Internet writers, defense lawyers, religious activists, and political dissidents. The activities of NGOs, especially those relating to the rule of law and public interest work, continue to be restricted. The Chinese Government also seeks to regulate religious groups and worship. Religious believers who seek to practice their faith outside of state-controlled religious venues and unregistered religious groups and spiritual movements are subject to intimidation, harassment, and detention. Chinese Communist Party members are discouraged from participating in religious activities.

Since 1999, the Secretary of State has designated China a "Country of Particular Concern" under the International Religious Freedom Act for particularly severe violations of religious freedom.

China's economic growth and reform since 1978 have improved economic conditions for hundreds of millions of Chinese, increased social mobility, and expanded the scope of personal freedom. This has meant greater freedom of travel, employment opportunities, educational and cultural pursuits, job and housing choices, and access to information. In April 2009 the government unveiled its first National Human Rights Action Plan. The document outlined human rights goals to be achieved in 2009 to 2010 and addressed issues such as prisoners' rights and the role of religion in society.

The U.S. has conducted 14 rounds of human rights dialogue with China since the Tiananmen massacre. The most recent round took place in April 2011, led by Assistant Secretary for Democracy, Human Rights and Labor Michael Posner and Chinese Ministry of Foreign Affairs Director General for International Organizations Chen Xu. Discussion topics included, but were not limited to, freedom of expression, rule of law, religious freedom, labor rights, minority issues, and multilateral cooperation.

On July 5, 2009, ethnic violence erupted in Urumqi and other parts of the Xinjiang Uighur Autonomous Region. The unrest continued in the following days, with Chinese state media reporting over 150 deaths and more than 1,000 injured. There was a significantly increased security presence in Urumqi and its surrounding areas and subsequently some mosques in Xinjiang were closed. Urumqi remains under a heavy police presence, and most Internet and international phone communication was cut off through early 2010.

On October 8, 2010 the independent Norwegian Nobel Committee awarded Chinese human rights activist Liu Xiaobo the Nobel Peace Prize "for his long and non-violent struggle for fundamental human rights in China." He was the first Chinese citizen awarded a Nobel Prize of any kind while residing in China. Liu Xiaobo was arrested in China in December 2008 and convicted of "incitement to subvert state power" in December 2009. He remains in prison. Since the announcement of the award of the 2010 Nobel Peace Prize, there have been consistent reports that his wife, Liu Xia, has been under de facto house arrest, with her movements and communication controlled by the authorities. The United States has repeatedly called for the immediate release of Liu Xiabo, as well as other political prisoners in China, including those under house arrest, such as Liu Xia, and those enduring forced disappearances, such as Gao Zhisheng.

In late 2010 and early 2011, dozens of people, including public interest lawyers, writers, artists, intellectuals, and activists were arbitrarily detained and arrested. Among them was the prominent artist Ai Weiwei, whose detention in early April 2011 signaled an expansion of the Chinese Government's crackdown on the activist community. While Ai Weiwei was released on bail in late June, the trend of forced disappearances, arbitrary detentions and arrests, and convictions of dissidents and activists in China for exercising their internationally recognized human rights continues.

China's Leaders:

Pres.
XI Jinping

Vice Pres.
LI Yuanchao

Premier, State Council
LI Keqiang

Executive Vice Premier, State Council
ZHANG Gaoli

Vice Premier, State Council
LIU Yandong

Vice Premier, State Council
WANG Yang

Vice Premier, State Council
MA Kai

State Councilor, State Council
YANG Jing

State Councilor, State Council
CHANG Wanquan

State Councilor, State Council
YANG Jiechi

State Councilor, State Council
GUO Shengkun

State Councilor, State Council
WANG Yong

Sec. Gen., State Council
YANG Jing

Chmn., Central Military Commission
XI Jinping

Chmn., National Development & Reform Commission
XU Shaoshi

Min. in Charge of the State Population & Family Planning Commission
LI Bin

Min. in Charge of the State Ethnic Affairs Commission
WANG Zhengwei

Min. of Agriculture
HAN Changfu

Min. of Civil Affairs
LI Liguo

Min. of Commerce
GAO Hucheng

Min. of Culture
CAI Wu

Min. of Education
YUAN Guiren

Min. of Environmental Protection
ZHOU Shengxian

Min. of Finance
LOU Jiwei

Min. of Foreign Affairs
WANG Yi

Min. of Housing & Urban-Rural Development
JIANG Weixin

Min. of Human Resources & Social Security
YIN Weimin

Min. of Industry & Information Technology
MIAO Wei

Min. of Justice
WU Aiying

Min. of Land & Resources
JIANG Daming

Min. of National Defense
CHANG Wanquan

Min. of Public Security
GUO Shengkun

Min. of Science & Technology
WAN Gang

Min. of State Security
GENG Huichang

Min. of Supervision
HUANG Shuxian

Min. of Transportation
YANG Chuantang

Min. of Water Resources
CHEN Lei

Auditor Gen., National Audit Office
LIU Jiayi

Governor, People's Bank of China
ZHOU Xiaochuan

Ambassador to the US
CUI Tiankai

Permanent Representative to the UN, New York
LIU   Jieyi

Economy

- GDP (2010 est.): $5.88 trillion (exchange rate-based); $10.09 trillion (purchasing power parity).

- Per capita GDP (2010): $7,600 (purchasing power parity).

- GDP real growth rate (2010): 10.3%.

- Natural resources: Coal, iron ore, petroleum, natural gas, mercury, tin, tungsten, antimony, manganese, molybdenum, vanadium, magnetite, aluminum, lead, zinc, uranium, hydropower potential (world's largest).

- Agriculture: Products--Among the world's largest producers of rice, wheat, potatoes, corn, peanuts, tea, millet, barley; commercial crops include cotton, other fibers, apples, oilseeds, pork and fish; produces variety of livestock products.

- Industry: Types--mining and ore processing, iron, steel, aluminum, and other metals, coal; machine building; armaments; textiles and apparel; petroleum; cement; chemicals; fertilizers; consumer products, including footwear, toys, and electronics; food processing; transportation equipment, including automobiles, rail cars and locomotives, ships, and aircraft; telecommunications equipment, commercial space launch vehicles, satellites.

- Trade Exports (2010)--$1.506 trillion: electrical and other machinery, including data processing equipment, apparel, textiles, iron and steel, optical and medical equipment. Main partners (2009)--U.S. 20.03%, Hong Kong 12.03%, Japan 8.32%, South Korea 4.55%, Germany 4.27%.

- Trade Imports (2010 est.)--$1.307 trillion: electrical and other machinery, oil and mineral fuels, optical and medical equipment, metal ores, plastics, organic chemicals. Main partners (2009)--Japan 12.27%, Hong

Kong 10.06%, South Korea 9.04%, U.S. 7.66%, Taiwan 6.84%, Germany 5.54%.

- Currency: Renminbi.

Economic Reforms

Since 1978, China has reformed and opened its economy. The Chinese leadership has adopted a more pragmatic perspective on many political and socioeconomic problems and has reduced the role of ideology in economic policy. China's ongoing economic transformation has had a profound impact not only on China but on the world. The market-oriented reforms China has implemented over the past 2 decades have unleashed individual initiative and entrepreneurship. The result has been the largest reduction of poverty and one of the fastest increases in income levels ever seen. In 2010, China overtook Japan to become the world's second-largest economy in terms of gross domestic product, behind the United States. It has sustained average economic growth of over 9.3% since 1989. In 2010 its $5.88 trillion economy was just over one-third the size of the U.S. economy.

China is firmly committed to economic reform and opening to the outside world. The Chinese leadership has identified reform of state industries, the establishment of a social safety net, reduction of the income gap, protection of the environment, and development of clean energy as government priorities. Government strategies for achieving these goals include large-scale privatization of unprofitable state-owned enterprises, development of a pension system for workers, establishment of an effective and affordable health care system, building environmental requirements into promotion criteria for government officials, and increasing rural incomes to allow domestic demand to play a greater role in driving economic growth. The leadership has also downsized the government bureaucracy.

In the 1980s, China tried to combine central planning with market-oriented reforms to increase productivity, living standards, and technological quality without exacerbating inflation, unemployment, and budget deficits. It pursued agricultural reforms, dismantling the commune system and introducing a household-based system that provided peasants greater decision-making in agricultural activities. The government also encouraged nonagricultural activities such as village enterprises in rural areas, promoted more self-management for state-owned enterprises, increased competition in the marketplace, and facilitated direct contact between Chinese and foreign trading enterprises. China also relied more upon foreign financing and imports.

During the 1980s, these reforms led to average annual growth rates of 10% in agricultural and industrial output. Rural per capita real income doubled. China became self-sufficient in grain production; rural industries accounted for 23% of agricultural output, helping absorb surplus labor in the countryside. The variety of light industrial and consumer goods increased. Reforms began in the fiscal, financial, banking, price-setting, and labor systems.

By the late 1980s, however, the economy had become overheated, with increasing rates of inflation. At the end of 1988, in reaction to a surge of inflation caused by accelerated price reforms, the leadership introduced an austerity program.

China's economy regained momentum in the early 1990s. During a visit to southern China in early 1992, China's paramount leader at the time, Deng Xiaoping, made a series of political pronouncements designed to reinvigorate the process of economic reform. The 14th Party Congress later in the year backed Deng's renewed push for market reforms, stating that China's key task in the 1990s was to create a "socialist market economy." The 10-year development plan for the 1990s stressed continuity in the political system with bolder reform of the economic system.

Following the Chinese Communist Party's October 2003 Third Plenum, Chinese legislators unveiled several proposed amendments to the state constitution. One of the most significant was a proposal to provide protection for private property rights. Legislators also indicated there would be a new emphasis on certain aspects of overall government economic policy, including efforts to reduce unemployment, which was officially 4.1% for urban areas in 2010 but is much higher when migrants are included. Other areas of emphasis include rebalancing income distribution between urban and rural regions and maintaining economic growth while protecting the environment and improving social equity. The National People's Congress approved the amendments when it met in March 2004. The Fifth Plenum in October 2005 approved the 11th Five-Year Plan aimed at building a "harmonious society" through more balanced wealth distribution and improved education, medical care, and social security. The 12th Five-Year Plan was debated in mid-October 2010 at the fifth plenary session of the 17th Central Committee of the CCP, and approved by the National People's Congress during its annual session in March 2011. The 12th Five-Year Plan seeks to transform China's development model from one reliant on exports and investment to a model based on domestic consumption. It also seeks to address rising inequality and create an environment for more sustainable growth by prioritizing more equitable wealth distribution, increased domestic consumption, and improved social infrastructure and social safety nets.

Agriculture

China is the world's most populous country and one of the largest producers and consumers of agricultural products. According to the UN World Food Program, in 2003, China fed 20% of the world's population with only 7% of the world's arable land (estimated at 121.7 million hectares in 2010, down from 129.9 million hectares in 1997). Almost 40% of China's labor force is engaged in agriculture, even though only 15% of the land is suitable for cultivation and agriculture contributes only about 10.3% of China's GDP (2009). China is among the world's largest producers of rice, corn, wheat, soybeans, vegetables, tea, and pork. Cotton is the major non-food commodity. China hopes to further increase agricultural production through improved plant stocks, fertilizers, new technologies (such as biotechnology), irrigation, and using more sustainable methods of production. The Chinese Government has also acknowledged that climate change poses a severe threat to the farming sector. Incomes for Chinese farmers are increasing more slowly than for urban residents, leading to an increasing wealth gap between the cities and countryside. Inadequate port facilities and a lack of warehousing and cold storage installations impede both domestic and international agricultural trade.

China is now one of the most important markets for U.S. exports; in 2010, U.S. exports to China totaled $91.9 billion, an all-time high. U.S. agricultural exports continue to play a major role in bilateral trade, totaling $17.9 billion in 2010 and thus making China the United States' largest agricultural export market. Leading categories include: soybeans ($11.3 billion), cotton ($1.988 billion), and hides and skins ($822 million).

Industry

Industry accounts for about 46.8% of China's GDP (2010 est.). Major industries are mining and ore processing; iron; steel; aluminum; coal; machinery; textiles and apparel; armaments; petroleum; cement; chemicals; fertilizers; consumer products including footwear, toys, and electronics; automobiles and other transportation equipment including rail cars and locomotives, ships, and aircraft; telecommunications equipment; commercial space launch vehicles; and satellites. China has become a preferred destination for the relocation of global manufacturing facilities. Its strength as an export platform has contributed to incomes and employment in China. The state-owned sector still accounts for about 40% of GDP (2010 est.). In recent years, authorities have been giving greater attention to the management of state assets--both in the financial market as well as among state-owned enterprises--and progress has been noteworthy.

Regulatory Environment

Though China's economy has expanded rapidly, its regulatory environment has not kept pace. Since Deng Xiaoping's open market reforms, the growth of new businesses has outpaced the government's ability to regulate them. This has created a situation where businesses, faced with mounting competition and poor oversight, will be willing to take drastic measures to increase profit margins, often at the expense of consumer safety. This issue acquired more prominence starting in 2007, with the United States placing a number of restrictions on problematic Chinese exports. The Chinese Government recognizes the severity of the problem, concluding in 2007 that nearly 20% of the country's products are substandard or tainted, and is undertaking efforts in coordination with the United States and others to better regulate the problem. The U.S. Food and Drug Administration (FDA) takes advantage of its presence in Beijing, Shanghai, and Guangzhou to monitor food safety issues, and in early 2011 the U.S. Consumer Product Safety

Commission opened its first-ever foreign office in Beijing to enhance cooperation and intensify exchanges with Chinese product safety regulators.

Energy

Driven by strong economic growth, China's demand for energy is surging rapidly. China is the world's largest energy consumer and the world's second-largest net importer of crude oil after the United States. China is also the fifth-largest energy producer in the world. The International Energy Agency estimates that China will contribute 36% to the projected growth in global energy use, with its demand rising by 75% between 2008 and 2035. China's electricity generation is expected to increase to 10,555 billion kilowatt hours (Bkwh) by 2035, over three times the amount in 2009, according to U.S. Energy Information Administration. In 2010, China led the world in clean energy investment with $51.1 billion and had installed wind capacity of 41.8 gigawatts, the most in the world.

Coal continues to make up the bulk of China's energy consumption (71% in 2009), and China is the largest producer and consumer of coal in the world. As China's economy continues to grow, China's coal demand is projected to rise significantly, although coal's share of China's overall energy consumption is expected to decrease. China's continued reliance on coal as a power source has contributed significantly to China's emergence as the world's largest emitter of acid rain-causing sulfur dioxide and green house gases, including carbon dioxide.

China's 12th Five-Year Plan (2011-2015) continues the government's policies encouraging greater energy conservation measures, development of renewable energy sources, and increased attention to environmental protection. China is exploring cleaner energy sources, including natural and shale gas, wind, solar, biomass, hydropower, and nuclear power, to reduce reliance on coal. China's renewable energy law calls for 15% of its energy to come from non-fossil fuel sources by 2020. In addition, the share of electricity generated by nuclear power is projected to grow from 1% in 2000 to 5% in 2020.

Since 1993, China has been a net importer of oil, a large portion of which comes from the Middle East. Net imports were approximately 4.3 million barrels per day in 2009. China's use of oil will continue to increase rapidly, particularly in response to the quick expansion of its vehicle fleets. Vehicle sales in China in 2010 rose 32% to over 18 million. China is interested in diversifying the sources of its oil imports and has invested in oil fields around the world. China recently concluded long-term loan-for-oil deals totaling $50 billion with Russia, Brazil, Venezuela, Kazakhstan, Angola, and Ecuador. In recent years, China's National Offshore Oil Corporation (CNOOC) has also invested in several U.S. oil and natural gas fields in Texas, Colorado, and Wyoming. Beijing also plans to increase China's natural gas use through imports and domestic production. Gas currently accounts for only 4% of China's total energy consumption. China has set an ambitious target of increasing the share of natural gas in its overall energy mix to 10%.

During the July 2009 inaugural meeting of the U.S.-China

Strategic and Economic Dialogue (S&ED), the two countries negotiated a memorandum of understanding (MOU) to enhance cooperation on climate change, energy, and the environment in order to expand and enhance cooperation on clean and efficient energy, to protect the environment, and to ensure energy security. The two sides also signed an MOU on cooperation on energy efficiency in buildings.

In November 2009, during President Barack Obama's state visit to China, the United States and China announced the establishment of the U.S.-China Clean Energy Research Center (CERC), which will focus on energy efficiency, clean coal including carbon capture and storage, and clean vehicles; signed the Renewable Energy Partnership; launched the U.S.-China Electric Vehicles Initiative; announced the bilateral Energy Efficiency Action Plan under the Ten-Year Framework on Energy and Environment; and inaugurated the U.S.-China Energy Cooperation Program, a public-private partnership focused on joint collaborative projects on renewable energy, smart grid, clean transportation, green building, clean coal, combined heat and power, and energy efficiency. The two countries also announced the launch of the U.S.-China Shale Gas Initiative, which will accelerate China's development of shale gas resources.

During President Hu's January 2011 state visit to the United States, the U.S. Department of Energy announced joint work plans under the U.S.-China CERC on building efficiency, clean coal, and clean vehicles, and started negotiations on a U.S.-China Eco-City Initiative to integrate energy efficiency and renewable energy into city design and operation in the two countries. In May 2011, the United States hosted the second U.S.-China Energy Efficiency Forum, and similar forums on biofuels and renewable energy are currently being planned.

Environment

One of the serious negative consequences of China's rapid industrial development has been increased pollution and degradation of natural resources. China surpassed the United

States as the world's largest emitter of carbon dioxide and other greenhouse gases in 2007. A World Health Organization report on air quality in 272 cities worldwide concluded that seven of the world's 10 most polluted cities were in China. According to China's own evaluation, two-thirds of the 338 cities for which air-quality data are available are considered polluted--two-thirds of those moderately or severely so. Almost all of the nation's rivers are considered polluted to some degree and half of the population lacks access to clean water. Ninety percent of urban bodies of water are severely polluted. Various studies estimate pollution costs the Chinese economy 7%-10% of GDP each year.

Water scarcity also is an issue, particularly in Northern China, where groundwater is being extracted at an increasingly unsustainable rate, seriously constricting future economic growth if stronger conservation measures are not taken or additional water not diverted. The central government is currently focused on the latter option, investing an estimated $60 billion in the South-North Water Diversion Project, a large-scale diversion of water from the Yangtze River to northern cities, including Beijing and Tianjin.

The question of environmental impacts associated with the Three Gorges Dam project has generated controversy among environmentalists inside and outside China. Critics claim that erosion and silting of the Yangtze River threaten several endangered species, while Chinese officials say the dam will help prevent devastating floods and generate clean hydroelectric power that will enable the region to lower its dependence on coal, thus lessening air pollution. There are also major concerns about whether water supply in the Yangtze is adequate to support the project.

China's leaders are increasingly paying attention to the country's severe environmental problems. In 1998, the State Environmental Protection Administration (SEPA) was officially upgraded to a ministry-level agency, the Ministry of Environmental Protection (MEP). In recent years, China has strengthened its environmental legislation and made some progress in stemming environmental deterioration. Beijing invested heavily in pollution control as part of its campaign to host a successful Olympiad in 2008, though some of the gains were temporary in nature. Some cities have seen improvement in air quality in recent years. The United States and China have been engaged in an active program of bilateral environmental cooperation since the mid-1990s, with a more recent emphasis on clean energy technology and the design of effective environmental policy. China has similar energy and environmental cooperation programs with Japan and European Union countries.

In 2008, China and the United States formed the Ten-Year Framework on Energy and Environment (TYF). The TYF facilitates the exchange of information and best practices between the two countries to foster innovation and develop solutions to the pressing energy and environment problems both countries face. The framework is comprised of seven action plans (clean air, clean water, clean and efficient transportation, clean and efficient electricity, energy efficiency, protected areas, and wetlands conservation) as well as the EcoPartnerships program, which seeks to encourage action plan collaboration at the sub-national level (states, cities, businesses, and universities) between the U.S. and China. Seven original EcoPartnerships were announced with the formation of the TYF in 2008, with six new partnerships signed during the third annual S&ED in May 2011.

During the July 2009 S&ED, the two countries negotiated an MOU to enhance cooperation on climate change, energy, and the environment, which further elaborated the role of the TYF and established a new dialogue and cooperation mechanism on climate change. During the May 2011 S&ED, the U.S. and China affirmed their efforts to work together to achieve a positive outcome at the UN Climate Change Conference in Durban, South Africa.

The first U.S.-China Renewable Energy Forum was held concurrently with the second annual S&ED in May 2010 in Beijing. Forums were held on energy efficiency, biofuels, and on promoting opportunities for U.S.-China collaboration to advance clean energy, including through $150 million in bilateral private and public funding for the CERC. Five-year work plans for the U.S. and Chinese CERC research teams were signed during President Hu Jintao's January 2011 visit.

In November 2010, U.S. and Chinese government officials convened the third meeting of the bilateral forum under the U.S.-China MOU on combating illegal logging and associated trade. During the meeting, the United States and China exchanged information on a variety of initiatives, including those with other countries, and explored ways to enhance bilateral cooperation. They discussed cooperation with the private sector and civil society in both countries and reviewed their experience with an ongoing trade data exchange. The delegations also reviewed outcomes from the meeting of the Asia-Pacific Regional Dialogue to Promote Trade in Legally Harvested Forest Products that was hosted by the U.S. in July. During the May 2011 S&ED, the U.S. and China agreed to hold the fourth bilateral forum on combating illegal logging and associated trade.

The U.S. Environmental Protection Agency (EPA) has cooperated with Chinese environmental agencies for many years, based on an MOU signed in 1980. In October 2010, EPA Administrator Lisa Jackson and Minister of Environmental Protection Zhou Shengxian signed a new MOU to expand cooperation across areas including water pollution and environmental law enforcement. The two agencies also co-chaired a session on electronic waste during the May 2011 S&ED.

China is an active participant in climate change talks and other multilateral environmental negotiations, taking environmental challenges seriously but pushing for the developed world to help developing countries. China is a member of the Major Economies Forum on Energy and Climate, and participates actively in the bilateral Climate Change Policy Dialogue. It signed on to the 2009 Copenhagen Accord in 2010 and inscribed a commitment to reducing its carbon intensity levels by 40%-45% by 2020 from 2005 levels. During President Hu's January 2011 visit, the U.S. and China agreed to implement the 2010 Cancun agreements and support efforts to achieve positive outcomes at the 2011 UN conference in South Africa.

China is a signatory to the Basel Convention governing the transport and disposal of hazardous waste and the Montreal Protocol for the Protection of the Ozone Layer, as well as the Convention on International Trade in Endangered Species and other major environmental agreements.

Water

Water scarcity is a critical issue in China. Recently, severe drought in northern China posed a serious threat to sustained economic growth and local livelihoods. Since the 1980s, China has experienced increased severity and frequency of water shortages due to variations in rainfall; excessive withdrawals of groundwater sources, polluted water resources, and inefficiencies in water usage. In normal water years, half of China's 662 cities have insufficient water supplies. Almost 94% of metropolitan areas with populations of more than one million people struggle to meet their annual water demands. Eleven percent of China's population lack access to improved drinking water sources (up from 33% in 1990); while 45% of the population lacks access to improved sanitation.

In addition, poor water quality continues to pose a challenge to environmental and human health. On a daily basis 300 million people drink contaminated water in China. Nine million cases of diarrhea linked to water pollution occur annually in China, based on China's 2003 National Health Survey. Approximately 61,000 people in China die annually from diarrhea related to polluted water--half of them are rural children.

The Government of China has responded to this crisis through large investments in the water sector, including storage, conveyance and treatment. Recent water and energy policies stressed conservation measures requiring municipalities and industry to consume less water. Large construction projects, such as the South-North Water Transfer project, are directed at addressing the water crisis. However, the question of environmental impacts associated with such projects has generated controversy among environmentalists inside and outside China. Critics assert that the magnitude and cost of building and operating large conveyance systems could result in unintended consequences that may overwhelm planned benefits. These consequences may include higher water prices, damage to local and downstream environments, additional treatment facilities for water that is currently too polluted to use, or further water shortages. China has announced its intention to funnel billions of renminbi of additional investment into water conservation projects during the 12th Five-Year Plan (2011-2015).

Science and Technology

Science and technology have always been a priority for China's leaders. Deng called it "the first productive force." Distortions in the economy and society created by party rule have severely hurt Chinese science, according to some Chinese science policy experts. The Chinese Academy of Sciences, modeled on the Soviet system, puts much of China's greatest scientific talent in a large, underfunded apparatus that remains largely isolated from industry, although the reforms of the past decade have begun to address this problem.

China is making significant investments in science and technology. Chinese science strategists see China's greatest opportunities in fields such as biotechnology and computers, where China is becoming an increasingly significant player. More overseas Chinese students are choosing to return home to work after graduation, and they have built a dense network of trans-Pacific contacts that will greatly facilitate U.S.-China scientific cooperation in coming years. The Chinese Government has increased incentives for students to return, such as salaries similar to those they would receive in the West. The U.S. space program is often held up as the standard of scientific modernity in China. China's small but growing space program, which successfully completed its third manned orbit in September 2008, is a focus of national pride. During National Aeronautics and Space Administration (NASA) Administrator Charles Bolden's October 2010 visit to China both sides agreed that transparency, reciprocity, and mutual benefit should serve as the foundation for future dialogue.

The U.S.-China Science and Technology Agreement remains the framework for bilateral cooperation in this field. During President Hu's January 2011 visit, the U.S. and China renewed the science and technology agreement, extending the framework for an additional 5 years. The agreement is among the longest-standing U.S.-China accords, and includes over 11 U.S. Federal agencies and numerous branches that participate in cooperative exchanges under the science and technology agreement and its nearly 60 protocols, memoranda of understanding, agreements, and annexes. The agreement covers cooperation in areas such as marine conservation, renewable energy, and health. Biennial Joint Commission Meetings on Science and Technology bring together policymakers from both sides to coordinate joint science and technology cooperation. Executive Secretaries meetings are held biennially to implement specific cooperation programs. Japan and the European Union also have high-profile science and technology cooperative relationships with China.

Trade

The U.S. trade deficit with China rose to $273.1 billion in 2010. This represents almost 55% of the total U.S. trade deficit. While U.S. exports to China grew by a third in 2010 to an all-time high of $91.9 billion, U.S. imports from China increased 23.1% to $364.9 billion. The top three U.S. exports to China in 2010 were electrical machinery ($11.5 billion), nuclear reactors and related machinery ($11.2 billion), and oil seeds and related products ($11 billion).

China remained the third-largest market for U.S. exports, accounting for 7.2% of U.S. goods exports in 2010. U.S. agricultural exports continue to play a major role in bilateral trade, totaling $17.9 billion in 2010 and thus making China the United States' largest agricultural export market. Leading categories include: soybeans ($11.3 billion), cotton ($1.988 billion), and hides and skins ($822 million).

Export growth continues to play an important role in China's rapid economic growth. To increase exports, China pursues policies such as fostering the rapid development of foreign-invested factories, which assemble imported components into consumer goods for export, and liberalizing trading rights. Since the adoption of the 11th Five-Year Program in 2005, however, China has placed greater emphasis on developing a consumer demand-driven economy to sustain economic growth and address global imbalances.

Foreign Investment

China's investment climate has changed dramatically in a quarter-century of reform. In the early 1980s, China restricted foreign investments to export-oriented operations and required foreign investors to form joint-venture partnerships with Chinese firms. Foreign direct investment (FDI) grew quickly during the 1980s, but slowed in late 1989 in the aftermath of Tiananmen. In response, the government introduced legislation and regulations designed to encourage foreigners to invest in high-priority sectors and regions. Since the early 1990s, China has allowed foreign investors to manufacture and sell a wide range of goods on the domestic market and authorized the establishment of wholly foreign-owned enterprises, now the preferred form of FDI. However, the Chinese Government's emphasis on guiding FDI into manufacturing has led to market saturation in some industries, while leaving China's services sectors underdeveloped. China is one of the leading FDI recipients in the world, receiving a record $105.7 billion in 2010 according to the Chinese Ministry of Commerce.

As part of its World Trade Organization (WTO) accession, China undertook to eliminate certain trade-related investment measures and to open up specified sectors that had previously been closed to foreign investment. Many new laws, regulations, and administrative measures to implement these commitments have been issued. Despite some reforms, major barriers to foreign investment remain, including restrictions on entire sectors, opaque and inconsistently enforced laws and regulations, and the lack of a rules-based legal infrastructure.

Opening to the outside remains central to China's development. Foreign-invested enterprises produce about half of China's exports, and China continues to attract large investment inflows. Foreign exchange reserves were $2.622 trillion at the end of 2010, and have now surpassed those of Japan, making China's foreign exchange reserves the largest in the world. As a result of its "going out" policy, China's outbound foreign direct investment, especially in energy and natural resources, has also surged in recent years, reaching $59 billion in 2010, up from a yearly average of $2 billion in the 1990s.

Foreign Relations

Since its establishment, the People's Republic has worked vigorously to win international support for its position that it is the sole legitimate government of all China, including Hong Kong, Macau, Tibet, and Taiwan. In the early 1970s, most world powers diplomatically recognized Beijing. Beijing assumed the China seat in the United Nations (UN) in 1971 and has since become increasingly active in multilateral organizations. Japan established diplomatic relations with China in 1972, and the United States did so in 1979. As of 2011, the number of countries that had diplomatic relations with Beijing had risen to 171, while 23 maintained diplomatic relations with Taiwan.

After the founding of the P.R.C., China's foreign policy initially focused on solidarity with the Soviet Union and other communist countries. In 1950, China sent the People's Liberation Army into North Korea to help North Korea halt the UN offensive that was approaching the Yalu River. After the conclusion of the Korean conflict, China sought to balance its identification as a member of the Soviet bloc by establishing friendly relations with Pakistan and other Third World countries, particularly in Southeast Asia.

In the 1960s, Beijing competed with Moscow for political influence among communist parties and in the developing world generally. Following the 1968 Soviet invasion of

Czechoslovakia and clashes in 1969 on the Sino-Soviet border, Chinese competition with the Soviet Union increasingly reflected concern over China's own strategic position.

In late 1978, the Chinese also became concerned over Vietnam's efforts to establish open control over Laos and Cambodia. In response to the Vietnamese invasion of Cambodia, China fought a brief border war with Vietnam (February-March 1979) with the stated purpose of "teaching Vietnam a lesson."

Chinese anxiety about Soviet strategic advances was heightened following the Soviet Union's December 1979 invasion of Afghanistan. Sharp differences between China and the Soviet Union persisted over Soviet support for Vietnam's continued occupation of Cambodia, the Soviet invasion of Afghanistan, and Soviet troops along the Sino-Soviet border and in Mongolia--the so-called "three obstacles" to improved Sino-Soviet relations.

In the 1970s and 1980s China sought to create a secure regional and global environment and to foster good relations with countries that could aid its economic development. To this end, China looked to the West for assistance with its modernization drive and for help in countering Soviet expansionism, which it characterized as the greatest threat to its national security and to world peace.

China maintained its consistent opposition to "superpower hegemony," focusing almost exclusively on the expansionist actions of the Soviet Union and Soviet proxies such as Vietnam and Cuba, but it also placed growing emphasis on a foreign policy independent of both the United States and the Soviet Union. While improving ties with the West, China continued to follow closely economic and other positions of the Third World nonaligned movement, although China was not a formal member.

In the immediate aftermath of Tiananmen crackdown in June 1989, many countries reduced their diplomatic contacts with China as well as their economic assistance programs. In response, China worked vigorously to expand its relations with foreign countries, and by late 1990, had reestablished normal relations with almost all nations. Following the collapse of the Soviet Union in late 1991, China also opened diplomatic relations with the republics of the former Soviet Union.

In recent years, Chinese leaders have been regular travelers to all parts of the globe, and China has sought a higher profile in the UN through its permanent seat on the United Nations Security Council and other multilateral organizations. Closer to home, China has made efforts to reduce tensions in Asia, hosting the Six-Party Talks on North Korea's nuclear weapons program. The United States and China share common goals of peace and stability on the Korean Peninsula and North Korean denuclearization. The U.S. continually consults with China on how it can best use its influence with North Korea and discusses the importance of fully implementing U.N. Security Council Resolutions 1718 and 1874, including sanctions to prevent North Korean proliferation activities.

China has cultivated a more cooperative relationship with members of the Association of Southeast Asian Nations

(ASEAN), and actively participated in the ASEAN Regional Forum. China has also taken steps to improve relations with countries in South Asia, including India, with which it has a longstanding border dispute. Marking the 60th year of diplomatic ties between the two countries, Premier Wen visited India in December 2010 to further develop the bilateral relationship between the two countries; trade in goods between the two countries reached nearly $60 billion in 2010. In April 2011, Prime Minister Manmohan Singh met President Hu on the margins of the Brazil, Russia, India and China (BRIC) Summit in Hainan.

China currently has warm ties with Russia, and President Hu chose Moscow for his first state visit after his assumption of office in 2003. China and Russia conducted a first round of joint military exercises in August 2005, and have since conducted regular joint exercises, often under the auspices of the Shanghai Cooperation Organization (SCO), a regional grouping that includes China, Russia, and the Central Asian nations of Kazakhstan, Kyrgyzstan, Tajikistan, and Uzbekistan.

Relations with Japan improved following Japanese Prime Minister Shinzo Abe's October 2006 visit to Beijing, and have seen a gradual improvement under successive Japanese administrations. Tensions persist with Japan, however, on longstanding and emotionally charged disputes over history and competing claims to portions of the East China Sea, and relations suffered a new dip following Japan's September 2010 arrest of a Chinese fishing trawler captain for ramming a Japanese Coast Guard vessel in the vicinity of the Japanese-administered Senkakus (Diaoyu) islands. A pause in tensions followed the March 11, 2011 earthquake and tsunami disaster, when China donated more than $4.5 million in humanitarian assistance and sent a 15-person search-and-rescue team to Japan--the first disaster team China had ever sent to Japan. In July 2011, Japan's then-Foreign Minister Takeaki Matsumoto visited Beijing for the first time since he had taken office.

Since 2000, Beijing has resolved territorial disputes by demarcating boundaries with Kazakhstan, Kyrgyzstan, Russia, Tajikistan, and Vietnam. Land boundary negotiations continue with Bhutan and India. China established a maritime boundary with Vietnam in the Gulf of Tonkin in 2000 but has no maritime boundaries in the Yellow Sea, East China Sea, and South China Sea, where it lays competing claims to islands and waters.

While it is one of Sudan's primary diplomatic patrons, China has played a constructive role in support of peacekeeping operations in the country and deployed 315 engineering troops in support of UN-African Union (AU) operations in Darfur. In January 2011, China sent a team of observers to Sudan to monitor the Southern Sudan referendum. In February 2011, the Ministry of Foreign Affairs stated China's respect for the referendum results as announced by the Southern Sudan Referendum Commission and expectations for the full implementation of the Comprehensive Peace Agreement (CPA). Following Southern Sudan's vote for secession, China maintained political relations with both Sudan and Southern Sudan, hosting the June 2011 visit of Sudanese President Omar al-Bashir to sign an oil and gas cooperation MOU. On July 9, 2011, after the official declaration of Independence by the Republic of South Sudan, China officially announced its recognition and its intent to promote peace and good relations between the north and south.

China has stated publicly that it shares the international community's concern over Iran's nuclear program and has voted in support of UN sanctions resolutions on Iran, most recently voting in favor of further sanctions on Iran in June 2010's UN Security Council Resolution 1929. The United States and China, both active participants in the "P5+1" process, called for Iran to fulfill its international obligations in a January 2011 joint statement. Set against these positive developments has been an effort on the part of China to maintain close ties to countries such as Iran, Sudan, Zimbabwe, and Venezuela that are sources of oil and other resources and which welcome China's non-conditional assistance and investment.

DEFENSE

The goal of establishing a professional military force equipped with modern weapons and doctrine took firm root when Deng Xiaoping made it part of China's official development strategy after consolidating power in 1978. In keeping with Deng's reform mandate, the People's Liberation Army (PLA), which is the consolidated military organization for China's land, sea, strategic missile, and air force, has demobilized millions of men and women since 1978 and introduced modern methods in such areas as recruitment and manpower, strategy, and education and training.

Following the June 1989 Tiananmen crackdown, ideological correctness was temporarily re-emphasized in Chinese military affairs. Reform and modernization appear to have since recovered their position as the PLA's priority objectives.

The Chinese military is in the process of transforming itself from a land-based power, centered on a vast ground force, to a smaller, mobile, high-tech military eventually capable of mounting limited operations beyond its coastal borders. China's power-projection capability is limited but has grown over recent years. China has acquired advanced weapons systems from abroad, including Sovremmeny destroyers, SU-27 and SU-30 aircraft, and Kilo-class diesel submarines from Russia. It continues to develop domestic production capabilities, such as for the domestically-developed J-10 fighter aircraft. In January 2011, China tested a prototype of its J-20 stealth fighter. Its first aircraft carrier began sea trials in August 2011. China has also modernized its strategic and conventional missile capabilities. However, much of its naval force continues to be based on 1960s-era technology. As the Defense Department's 2010 Quadrennial Defense Review noted, the United States welcomes the positive benefits that can accrue from greater cooperation with China, but has questions about the lack of transparency surrounding China's military modernization plans. The United States has repeatedly called for China to provide greater transparency about its capabilities and intentions, and the U.S. views military exchanges, visits, and other forms of engagement as useful tools in advancing this goal. Regularized exchanges and contact also have the significant benefit of building confidence, reducing the possibility of accidents, and improving communication in order to reduce the risk of misperceptions and miscalculations. During President Hu's January 2011 visit, President Obama and President Hu issued a joint statement that reaffirmed the essential role of a "healthy, stable, and reliable military-to-military relationship," and agreed on the need for enhanced and substantive dialogue and communication at all levels. U.S. and Chinese militaries are also considering ways in which the two countries might cooperate on humanitarian assistance, disaster relief, counter-piracy, and peacekeeping operations.

China became a major international arms exporter during the 1980s. Beijing joined the Middle East arms control talks, which began in July 1991 to establish global guidelines for conventional arms transfers, but announced in September 1992 that it would no longer participate because of the U.S. decision to sell F-16A/B aircraft to Taiwan.

Nuclear Weapons

In 1955, Mao Zedong's Chinese Communist Party decided to proceed with a nuclear weapons program; it was developed with Soviet assistance until the Sino-Soviet split ended that assistance. After its first nuclear test in October 1964, Beijing deployed a modest but potent ballistic missile force, including land- and sea-based intermediate-range and intercontinental ballistic missiles.

China maintains an official nuclear doctrine of "no first use" of nuclear weapons. It joined the International Atomic Energy Agency (IAEA) in 1984 and pledged to abstain from further atmospheric testing of nuclear weapons in 1986. China acceded to the nuclear Non-Proliferation Treaty (NPT) in 1992 and supported its indefinite and unconditional extension in 1995. In 1996, it signed the Comprehensive Test Ban Treaty (CTBT) and agreed to seek an international ban on the production of fissile nuclear weapons material. As of July 2011, China had not yet ratified the CTBT, though in their November 2009 meeting, President Obama and President Hu committed to pursue ratification of the CTBT as soon as possible and to work together for its early entry into force.

In 1996, China committed to not providing assistance to unsafeguarded nuclear facilities. It became a full member of the NPT Exporters (Zangger) Committee, a group that determines items subject to IAEA inspections if exported by NPT signatories. In September 1997, China issued detailed nuclear export control regulations. It began implementing regulations establishing controls over nuclear-related dual-use items in 1998. China also has committed not to engage in new nuclear cooperation with Iran (even under safeguards), and will complete existing cooperation, which is not of proliferation concern, within a relatively short period. In May 2004, with the support of the United States, China became a member of the Nuclear Suppliers Group.

In April 2010, President Hu Jintao attended the Nuclear Security Summit, hosted by President Obama in Washington,

DC. The summit focused on how to better safeguard weapons-grade plutonium and uranium to prevent nuclear terrorism. At the summit, China agreed to work with the United States at the United Nations on a resolution imposing further economic sanctions on Iran. In January 2011, the United States and China signed a memorandum of understanding to help establish a Center of Excellence on Nuclear Security in China.

Chemical Weapons

China is not a member of the Australia Group, an informal and voluntary arrangement created in 1985 to monitor developments in the proliferation of dual-use chemicals and to coordinate export controls on key dual-use chemicals and equipment with weapons applications. In April 1997, however, China ratified the Chemical Weapons Convention (CWC) and, in September 1997, promulgated a new chemical weapons export control directive. In 2002 and 2005, China promulgated updated regulations on dual-use chemical and biological agents and equipment, thereby controlling all the major items on the Australia Group's control list. The U.S. continues to see proliferation activity by some Chinese entities, however, which has resulted in sanctions against these companies.

Missiles

China is not a member of the Missile Technology Control Regime (MTCR), a multinational effort to restrict the proliferation of missiles. But in March 1992, China undertook measures to abide by MTCR guidelines and parameters. China reaffirmed this commitment in 1994, and pledged not to transfer MTCR-class ground-to-ground missiles. In November 2000, China committed not to assist in any way the development by other countries of missiles capable of delivering a 500-kilogram (kg) payload to range of 300 kilometers (km). In December 2003, the P.R.C. promulgated comprehensive new export control regulations governing exports of all categories of sensitive technologies. The U.S.

continues to seek ways to work with China to strengthen its implementation and enforcement of rigorous export controls for missile technology.

U.S- China Relations

From Revolution to the Shanghai Communique

As the PLA armies moved south to complete the communist conquest of China in 1949, the American Embassy followed the Nationalist government headed by Chiang Kai-shek, finally moving to Taipei later that year. U.S. consular officials remained in mainland China. The new P.R.C. Government was hostile to this official American presence, and all U.S. personnel were withdrawn from the mainland in early 1950. Any remaining hope of normalizing relations ended when U.S. and Chinese communist forces fought on opposing sides in the Korean conflict.

Beginning in 1954 and continuing until 1970, the United States and China held 136 meetings at the ambassadorial level, first in Geneva and later in Warsaw. In the late 1960s, U.S. and Chinese political leaders decided that improved bilateral relations were in their common interest. In 1969, the United States initiated measures to relax trade restrictions and other impediments to bilateral contact. On July 15, 1971, President Nixon announced that his Assistant for National Security Affairs, Henry Kissinger, had made a secret trip to Beijing to initiate direct contact with the Chinese leadership and that he, the President, had been invited to visit China.

In February 1972, President Nixon traveled to Beijing, Hangzhou, and Shanghai. At the conclusion of his trip, the U.S. and Chinese Governments issued the "Shanghai Communique," a statement of their foreign policy views.

In the Communique, both nations pledged to work toward the full normalization of diplomatic relations. The United States acknowledged the Chinese position that all Chinese on both sides of the Taiwan Strait maintain that there is only one China and that Taiwan is part of China. The statement enabled the United States and China to temporarily set aside the "crucial question obstructing the normalization of relations"--Taiwan-- and to open trade and other contacts.

Liaison Office, 1973-1978

In May 1973, in an effort to build toward the establishment of formal diplomatic relations, the United States and China established the United States Liaison Office (USLO) in Beijing and a counterpart Chinese office in Washington, DC. In the years between 1973 and 1978, such distinguished Americans as David Bruce, George H.W. Bush, Thomas Gates, and Leonard Woodcock served as chiefs of the USLO with the personal rank of Ambassador.

President Ford visited China in 1975 and reaffirmed the U.S. interest in normalizing relations with Beijing. Shortly after taking office in 1977, President Carter again reaffirmed the interest expressed in the Shanghai Communique. The United States and China announced on December 15, 1978, that the two governments would establish diplomatic relations on January 1, 1979.

Normalization

In the Joint Communique on the Establishment of Diplomatic Relations dated January 1, 1979, the United States transferred diplomatic recognition from Taipei to Beijing. The United States reiterated the Shanghai Communique's acknowledgment of the Chinese position that there is only one China and that Taiwan is a part of China; Beijing acknowledged that the American people would continue to carry on commercial, cultural, and other unofficial contacts with the people of Taiwan. The Taiwan Relations Act made the necessary changes in U.S. domestic law to permit such unofficial relations with Taiwan to flourish.

U.S.-China Relations since Normalization

Vice Premier Deng Xiaoping's January 1979 visit to

Washington, DC, initiated a series of important, high-level exchanges, which continued until the spring of 1989. This resulted in many bilateral agreements--especially in the fields of scientific, technological, and cultural interchange and trade relations. Since early 1979, the United States and China have initiated hundreds of joint research projects and cooperative programs under the Agreement on Cooperation in Science and Technology, the largest bilateral program.

On March 1, 1979, the United States and China formally established embassies in Beijing and Washington, DC. During 1979, a bilateral trade agreement was concluded. Vice President Walter Mondale reciprocated Vice Premier Deng's visit with an August 1979 trip to China. This visit led to agreements in September 1980 on maritime affairs, civil aviation links, and textile matters, as well as a bilateral consular convention.

As a consequence of high-level and working-level contacts initiated in 1980, U.S.-China dialogue broadened to cover a wide range of issues, including global and regional strategic problems, political-military questions, arms control, UN and other multilateral organization affairs, and international narcotics matters.

The expanding relationship was threatened in 1981 by Chinese objections to the level of U.S. arms sales to Taiwan. Secretary of State Alexander Haig visited China in June 1981 in an effort to resolve Chinese questions about America's unofficial relations with Taiwan. Eight months of negotiations produced the U.S.-China joint communique of August 17, 1982. In this third communique, the United States stated its intention, if conditions were conducive, to reduce gradually the level of arms sales to Taiwan, and the Chinese described as a fundamental policy their effort to strive for a peaceful resolution to the Taiwan question. Meanwhile, Vice President George H.W. Bush visited China in May 1982.

High-level exchanges continued to be a significant means for developing U.S.-China relations in the 1980s. President Reagan and Premier Zhao Ziyang made reciprocal visits in 1984. In July 1985, President Li Xiannian traveled to the United States, the first such visit by a Chinese head of state. Vice President

Bush visited China in October 1985 and opened the U.S. Consulate General in Chengdu, the fourth U.S. consular post in China. Further exchanges of cabinet-level officials occurred between 1985 and 1989, capped by President George H.W. Bush's visit to Beijing in February 1989.

In the period before the June 3-4, 1989 crackdown, a large and growing number of cultural exchange activities undertaken at all levels exposed the American and Chinese people to each other's cultural, artistic, and educational achievements. Numerous Chinese professional and official delegations visited the United States each month. Many of these exchanges continued after Tiananmen.

Bilateral Relations After Tiananmen

Following the Chinese authorities' brutal suppression of demonstrators in June 1989, the United States and other governments enacted a number of measures to express their condemnation of China's blatant violation of basic human rights. The United States suspended high-level official exchanges with China and weapons exports from the United States to China. The United States also imposed a number of economic sanctions. In the summer of 1990, at the G-7 Houston Summit, Western nations called for renewed political and economic reforms in China, particularly in the field of human rights.

Tiananmen disrupted the U.S.-China trade relationship, and U.S. investors' interest in China dropped dramatically. The U.S. Government also responded to the political repression by suspending certain trade and investment programs on June 5 and 20, 1989. Some sanctions were legislated; others were executive actions. Examples include:

- The U.S. Trade and Development Agency (TDA)--new activities in China were suspended from June 1989 until January 2001, when President Bill Clinton lifted this suspension.

- Overseas Private Insurance Corporation (OPIC)--new activities suspended since June 1989.
- Development Bank Lending/IMF Credits--the United States does not support development bank lending and will not support IMF credits to China except for projects that address basic human needs.
- Munitions List Exports--subject to certain exceptions, no licenses may be issued for the export of any defense article on the U.S. Munitions List. This restriction may be waived upon a presidential national interest determination.
- Arms Imports--import of defense articles from China was banned after the imposition of the ban on arms exports to China. The import ban was subsequently waived by the Administration and re-imposed on May 26, 1994. It covers all items on the Bureau of Alcohol, Tobacco, Firearms, and Explosives' Munitions Import List.

In 1996, the P.R.C. conducted military exercises in waters close to Taiwan in an apparent effort at intimidation, after Taiwan's former President, Lee Teng-huei, made a private visit to the

United States. The United States dispatched two aircraft carrier battle groups to the region. Subsequently, tensions in the Taiwan Strait diminished, and relations between the United States and China improved, with increased high-level exchanges and progress on numerous bilateral issues, including human rights, nonproliferation, and trade. Chinese president Jiang Zemin visited the United States in the fall of 1997, the first state visit to the United States by a Chinese president since 1985. In connection with that visit, the two sides reached agreement on implementation of their 1985 agreement on peaceful nuclear cooperation. President Clinton visited China in June 1998. He traveled extensively in China, interacting directly with the Chinese people through live speeches, press conference, and a radio show, which allowed the President to convey first-hand to the Chinese people a sense of American ideals and values.

Relations between the United States and China were severely strained by the tragic accidental bombing of the Chinese Embassy in Belgrade in May 1999. By the end of 1999, relations began to gradually improve and in October 1999, the two sides reached agreement on humanitarian payments for families of those who died and those who were injured as well as payments for damages to respective diplomatic properties in Belgrade and China. Relations cooled again in April 2001, when a Chinese F-8 fighter collided with a U.S. EP-3 reconnaissance aircraft flying over international waters south of China. The EP-3 was able to make an emergency landing on China's Hainan Island despite extensive damage; the P.R.C. aircraft crashed with the loss of its pilot. Following extensive negotiations, the crew of the EP-3 was allowed to leave China 11 days later, but the U.S. aircraft was not permitted to depart for another 3 months.

Relations gradually improved and President George W. Bush visited China in February 2002 and met with President Jiang Zemin in Crawford, Texas in October. President Bush hosted Premier Wen Jiabao in Washington in December 2003. President Bush first met Hu Jintao in his new capacity as P.R.C. President on the margins of the G-8 Summit in Evian in June 2003. President Obama and President Hu have met nine times, most recently during President Hu's January 2011 visit--the first state visit of a Chinese leader to the United States since 1997. President Obama first met with President Hu during the London G20 Summit in April 2009. President Obama has met with Premier Wen three times, most recently on the sidelines of the UN General Assembly in September 2010.

U.S. China policy has been consistent. For eight consecutive administrations, Democratic and Republican, U.S. policy has been to encourage China's opening and integration into the global system. As a result, China has moved from being a relatively isolated and poor country to a key participant in international institutions and a major trading nation. The United States encourages China to play an active role as a responsible stakeholder in the international community, working with the United States and other countries to support and strengthen the international system that has enabled China's success. In the words of Secretary Hillary Clinton, the U.S. wants to "develop a positive, cooperative, and comprehensive relationship with China." Senior State Department officials engage in regular and intensive discussions with their P.R.C. counterparts through the U.S.-China Strategic and Economic Dialogue.

China plays an important role in global, regional, and bilateral counterterrorism efforts, and supports coalition efforts in Afghanistan and Iraq. Following the September 11, 2001 terrorist attacks (9-11) in New York City and Washington, DC, China offered strong public support against terrorism and served as an important partner in U.S. counterterrorism efforts. Shortly after 9-11, the United States and China also commenced a Counterterrorism Sub-Dialogue, conducting its seventh round of talks in September 2009. Inspections under the Container Security Initiative (CSI) are now underway at the major ports of Shenzhen, Shanghai, and Hong Kong. China also agreed to participate in the Department of Energy's Megaports Initiative, a critical part of U.S. efforts to detect the flow of nuclear materials. China voted in favor of UN Security Council Resolution 1373 on counterterrorism, publicly supported the coalition campaign in Afghanistan, and contributed $150 million of bilateral assistance to Afghan reconstruction following the defeat of the Taliban. China participated in both the Iraq Neighbors and International Compact with Iraq meetings in 2007 and voiced strong support for the Government of Iraq following the country's December 2005 parliamentary elections. China in 2003 pledged $25 million to Iraqi reconstruction and has taken measures to forgive Iraq's sovereign debt to China.

The United States and China continue to cooperate with growing effectiveness on various aspects of law enforcement, including computer crime, intellectual property rights enforcement, human smuggling, and corruption. The most recent meeting of the U.S.-China Joint Liaison Group (JLG) on law enforcement cooperation took place in November 2010.

China and the United States are also working closely with the international community to address threats to global security, including North Korea and Iran's nuclear programs. China played a constructive role in hosting the Six-Party Talks and in brokering the February 2007 agreement on Initial Actions. The United States looks to Beijing to use its unique position with Pyongyang to convince North Korea to cease its provocative behavior and to ensure that it implements fully its commitments under the September 2005 Joint Statement of the Six-Party

Talks and relevant UN Security Council resolutions. In the January 2011 U.S.-China joint statement, the United States and China expressed concern regarding North Korea's claimed uranium enrichment program and agreed on the crucial importance of denuclearization of the Korean Peninsula. China has publicly stated that it does not want Iran to acquire nuclear weapons and has voted in support of sanctions resolutions on Iran at the UN Security Council. On these and other important issues, such as the ongoing humanitarian crisis in Darfur, the United States expects China to join with the international community in finding solutions. China's participation is critical to efforts to combat transnational health threats such as avian influenza and HIV/AIDS, and both the United States and China play an important role in new multilateral energy initiatives, such as the Asia-Pacific Partnership.

While the United States looks forward to building a positive, cooperative, and comprehensive relationship with China--a message reiterated by President Obama during President Hu's January 2011 visit--areas of potential disagreement remain. The Obama Administration welcomes the impressive steps taken on both sides of the Taiwan Strait to improve relations, and hopes these efforts will expand. The United States remains committed to its one China policy based on the three joint communiqués and the Taiwan Relations Act.

U.S.-China Economic Relations

U.S. direct investment in China covers a wide range of manufacturing sectors, several large hotel projects, restaurant chains, and petrochemicals. U.S. companies have entered agreements establishing more than 20,000 equity joint ventures, contractual joint ventures, and wholly foreign-owned enterprises in China. More than 100 U.S.-based multinationals have projects in China, some with multiple investments. U.S. foreign direct investment in China was $60 billion in 2010.

The United States is one of China's primary suppliers of power-generating equipment, aircraft and parts, computers and industrial machinery, raw materials, pharmaceuticals and chemical and agricultural products. However, U.S. exporters continue to have concerns about protection of intellectual property rights, fair market access due to testing and standards that do not necessarily correspond with international standards and policies that pursue import substitution. In addition, a lack of transparency in the regulatory and rule-making process makes it difficult for businesses to plan for changes in the domestic market structure.

Total two-way trade between China and the United States grew from $33 billion in 1992 to over $456 billion in 2010. The United States is China's second-largest trading partner (after the EU), and China is now the third-largest trading partner for the United States (after the EU and Canada). U.S. exports to China have been growing more rapidly than to any other market, reaching $114 billion in 2010 ($93 billion in goods and $21 billion in services), and U.S. imports from China accounted for 19% of overall U.S. imports in 2009. The U.S. trade deficit with China in 2010 rose to $273.1 billion. Some of the factors that influence the U.S. trade deficit with China include:

- A recent trend has shifted low-end assembly industries to China from the newly industrialized economies (NIEs) in Asia. China now serves as the last link in a long chain of value-added production. Because U.S. trade data attributes the full value of a product to the final assembler, Chinese value-added gets over-counted.
- China's restrictive trade practices, which include an array of barriers to foreign goods and services, are often aimed at protecting state-owned enterprises. Under its WTO accession agreement, China is reducing tariffs, eliminating import licensing requirements, and addressing other trade barriers.

The U.S. approach to its economic relations with China has two main elements. First, the United States seeks to fully integrate China into the global, rules-based economic and trading system. China's participation in the global economy will nurture the process of economic reform, encourage China to take on responsibilities commensurate with its growing influence, and increase China's stake in the stability and prosperity of East Asia and the rest of the world.

Second, the United States seeks to expand U.S. exporters' and investors' access to the Chinese market. As China grows and develops, its needs for imported goods and services will rapidly grow. The U.S. Government will continue to work with China's leadership to ensure full and timely conformity with China's WTO commitments--including effective protection of intellectual property rights--and to encourage China to move to a flexible, market-based exchange rate in order to further increase U.S. exports of goods, agricultural products, and services to the P.R.C.

In December 2010, the United States and China convened the 21st session of the Joint Commission on Commerce and Trade (JCCT), co-chaired by then-Secretary of Commerce Gary Locke, U.S. Trade Representative Ron Kirk, and Vice Premier Wang Qishan in Hangzhou, China. The two sides addressed a range of issues, and positive results included China's commitments to enhance its enforcement of intellectual property rights, adopt non-discriminatory government procurement policies, and collaborate with the U.S. in areas of emerging technology such as Smart Grid. China's commitments will lead to increased opportunities for U.S. exporters and a more level playing field for U.S. companies operating in China. The JCCT will next be convened in China in the fall of 2011.

U.S.-China Strategic and Economic Dialogue (S&ED)

During a discussion of U.S.-China relations and global issues of common interest at a bilateral meeting in April 2009, President Obama and President Hu agreed to work toward a positive, cooperative, and comprehensive U.S.-China relationship for the 21st century. They established the U.S.-China Strategic and Economic Dialogue as a mechanism to realize that goal.

The Strategic and Economic Dialogue (S&ED), which brings together the top foreign and economic policy officials from both countries, provides a framework for the U.S. and China to discuss bilateral, regional, and global issues of common concern, identify potential areas of cooperation, address differences frankly, and build mutual trust. This whole-of-government approach reinforces and helps to coordinate the many existing bilateral dialogues that the U.S. has with China.

On July 27-28, 2009, the inaugural Strategic and Economic Dialogue was held in Washington, DC and was led by four co-chairs: Secretary of State Clinton, Treasury Secretary Timothy Geithner, Vice Premier Wang Qishan, and State Councilor Dai Bingguo. The second S&ED was held May 24-25, 2010 in Beijing, and the third S&ED took place May 9-10, 2011 in Washington, DC. The co-chairs remained unchanged in the second and third rounds.

The S&ED is divided into strategic and economic track discussions. At the strategic track of the third S&ED led by Secretary Clinton and State Councilor Dai, the two sides discussed bilateral relations (including human rights, military-to-military relations, and Taiwan), international security issues (including nonproliferation, UN peacekeeping, and maritime security), global issues (including health, climate change, and energy) and specific regional issues (including Sudan,

Afghanistan/Pakistan, Iran, and North Korea). They also announced the establishment of the U.S.-China Strategic Security Dialogue (SSD) under the strategic track of the S&ED, and held the inaugural round of the SSD.

The economic track, led by Secretary Geithner and Vice Premier Wang, discussed promoting strong, sustainable, and balanced growth; strengthening financial systems; and enhancing trade and investment cooperation.

Key Names and Contacts

Principal Government and Party Officials

- President--Hu Jintao

- Vice President--Xi Jinping

- Premier, State Council--Wen Jiabao

- State Councilors--Liu Yandong, Liang Guanglie, Ma Kai, Meng Jianzhu, Dai Bingguo

- Secretary General--Ma Kai

- NPC Chair--Wu Bangguo

- Vice Premiers--Li Keqiang, Hui Liangyu, Zhang Dejiang, Wang Qishan

- Politburo Standing Committee--Hu Jintao (General Secretary), Wu Bangguo, Wen Jiabao, Jia Qinglin, Li Changchun, Xi Jinping, Li Keqiang, He Guoqiang, Zhou Yongkang

- Other Politburo Members--Bo Xilai, Guo Boxiong, Hui Liangyu, Li Yuanchao, Liu Qi, Liu Yandong, Liu Yunshan, Wang Gang, Wang Lequan, Wang Qishan, Wang Zhaoguo, Xu Caihou, Yu Zhengsheng, Zhang Dejiang, Zhang Gaoli, Wang Yang

- Chairman, Central Military Commission--Hu Jintao

- Minister of Foreign Affairs--Yang Jiechi

- Minister of Commerce--Chen Deming

- Minister of Finance--Xie Xuren

- Minister of Agriculture--Han Changfu

- Minister of Information Industry--Li Yizhong

- Minister of Public Security--Meng Jianzhu

- Minister of State Security--Geng Huichang

- Minister of Science and Technology Wan Gang

- Minister of Justice--Minister Wu Aiying

- Prosecutor General--Cao Jianming

- Governor, People's Bank of China--Zhou Xiaochuan

- Minister, State Development and Reform Commission--Zhang Ping

- Ambassador to the United States--Zhang Yesui

- Ambassador to the United Nations, New York--Li Baodong

- Ambassador to the United Nations, Geneva--He Yafei

American Diplomatic Representation in China

Gary Locke
U.S. Ambassador to China
American Embassy Beijing
No. 55 An Jia Lou Road
Beijing 100600
People's Republic of China
Tel.: (86) (10) 8531-3000

On March 9, 2011, President Barack Obama nominated Gary Locke to be Ambassador of the United States of America to

China. He was confirmed by the Senate on July 27, 2011 and was sworn in on August 1, 2011.

Previously, Ambassador Locke served as the Secretary of Commerce where he helped implement President Obama's ambitious agenda to turn around the economy and put people back to work. As the administration's point person for achieving the President's National Export Initiative, Ambassador Locke presided over a 17 percent increase in exports, compared to 2009. Before his appointment to the President's Cabinet, Ambassador Locke served two terms as Governor of Washington, the nation's most trade-dependent state. He expanded the sale of Washington products and services by leading 10 productive trade missions to Asia, Mexico and Europe. During the eight years of the Locke administration, Washington state gained 280,000 jobs despite two national recessions.

Along with his longstanding commitment to public service, Ambassador Locke has extensive experience working with China. As Secretary of Commerce, he co-chaired two sessions of the U.S.-China Joint Commission on Commerce and Trade that resulted in important changes to Chinese trade policy, helping to level the playing field for U.S. businesses exporting to and operating in China. He also led a clean energy mission to China and Indonesia. As Governor of Washington, he successfully strengthened economic ties between China and Washington state, more than doubling the state's exports to China to over $5 billion per year. As a partner in the Seattle office of the international law firm, Davis Wright Tremaine LLP, he co-chaired the firm's China practice.

Ambassador Locke is the first Chinese-American to serve in any of the above government posts. His grandfather emigrated from China to Washington state, initially finding employment as a servant, working in exchange for English lessons. His father, also born in China, was a small business owner, operating a grocery store where Ambassador Locke worked while receiving his education from Seattle's public school system.

Ambassador Locke earned a bachelor's degree in political science from Yale University and a law degree from Boston University. He is married and has three children.

In addition to the U.S. Embassy in Beijing, there are U.S. Consulates General in Chengdu, Guangzhou, Shanghai, Shenyang, and Wuhan.

Chinese Diplomatic Representation in the United States

Ambassador Zhang Yesui
Embassy of the People's Republic of China
3505 International Place, NW
Washington, DC 20008
Tel.: (202) 495-2266

In addition to China's embassy in Washington, DC, there are Chinese Consulates General in Chicago, Houston, Los Angeles, New York, and San Francisco.

Consulate General of the People's Republic of China

New York
520 12th Avenue
New York, NY 10036
Tel.: (212) 244-9456

Consulate General of the People's Republic of China
San Francisco
1450 Laguna Street
San Francisco, California 94115
Tel.: (415) 674-2905

Consulate General of the People's Republic of China
Houston
3417 Montrose Blvd.
Houston, Texas 77006
Tel.: (713) 520-1462

Consulate General of the People's Republic of China
Chicago
100 West Erie St.
Chicago, Illinois 60610

Tel.: (312) 803-0095

Consulate General of the People's Republic of China
Los Angeles
502 Shatto Place, Suite 300
Los Angeles, California 90020
Tel.: (213) 807-8088

The Internationalist®
International Business, Investment, and Travel

www.internationalist.com

www.ingramcontent.com/pod-product-compliance
Lightning Source LLC
Chambersburg PA
CBHW051716170526
45167CB00002B/686